Letters to My Daughters ♥♥♥♥

Seven Truths Every Woman Should Know

BRENNA MᶜLENNAN

ELECTRIC
MOON
PUBLISHING

Electric Moon Publishing, LLC
P.O. Box 466
Stromsburg, NE 68666
info@emoonpublishing.com

Scripture taken from the NEW AMERICAN STANDARD BIBLE®, Copyright © 1960, 1962, 1963, 1968, 1971, 1972, 1973, 1975, 1977, 1995 by The Lockman Foundation. Used by permission.

Edited by Lee Warren and Becky Swanberg / Electric Moon Publishing Editorial Services
Cover image courtesy of Matt Reaves
Cover and Interior Design by Lyn Rayn / Electric Moon Publishing Creative Services

Printed in the United States of America

ELECTRIC MOON PUBLISHING
www.emoonpublishing.com

Contents

DEDICATION

To my dear husband, Tanner—the love of my life and the absolute best father to our girls. How I wish you could see through my eyes for just a second!

♥ ♥ ♥ ♥

To my dear daughters, Maddie, Amy, Maebree, and Adalyn—the ones who bring me more joy than I ever thought possible. Each one of you is oh so special, and you are loved beyond measure!

♥ ♥ ♥ ♥

To my very own dear mother—the one who laid the first brick. Thank you for living out a lifetime of faith in front of me! May our LORD bless you!

Dear Daughters,

♥ ♥ ♥♥

*I*t started when our third daughter was born. Well-meaning people jokingly, and maybe not-so-jokingly, warned us about the expense, the drama, and the weddings that were to come. When our fourth daughter came along, we became the parents of four daughters in six years—yes, you read that right. From that moment on, we have constantly found ourselves receiving curious looks from strangers, helpful hints about elopements, raised eyebrows with warnings about their teenage years, and many questions about our desire for a boy, whether they are all ours, and even our possession of a TV.

"Wow! Your hands are full."

"You've got lots of helpers!"

"*All* girls? I feel so sorry for you."

"Your poor husband."

"That's a bunch of pretty little girls!"

"I'll pray for you . . ."

"You're so blessed to have daughters!"

That last one I love. Oh, how blessed we are.

On a recent trip with our blessings, I watched as their uncle took a picture of the four of them holding hands and looking away from our family. Unexpectedly and all at once, exceeding joy and nagging doubt washed over my heart.

Joy—in watching these four young girls lock hands with each other. They truly do love one another, and by God's great grace, they have each other to hold onto.

Doubt—as the reality of their future also came to mind. There will be a day, not too far off, when each one will look away from our family and go out into the world.

Like any parent, I assume, I struggle—always questioning whether I am doing enough, teaching enough, laying enough of a foundation for these precious gifts. These questions began when our first little girl was born, and as each daughter has been added and each year passes, the questions still rise.

From the moment I found out we were having a daughter, I knew I'd been tasked with preparing her for the onslaught of challenges and falsehoods that the world would throw at her. Now, as I look at this picture, I see a world that is quickly changing, growing more difficult to navigate and more evil at a pace I can't seem to keep up with, and my concerns grow in step. I see an abundance of lies, mistruths, and deceptions which will try to lead her astray.

A saying floats around on social media that says, "If we don't teach our children to follow Christ, the world will teach them not to." As much as I agree with this, I would like to change it a little: "*Even if* we teach our children to follow Christ, the world will still teach them not to." Or maybe, "*As* we teach our children to follow Christ, the world is teaching them not to."

Make no mistake, this world is not neutral. It is absolutely opposed to Jesus Christ and His Gospel. His disciples are promised trouble, hardship, and suffering as they stand for Him—for the Truth. As Christian parents, we must constantly be teaching our children to follow Christ because this world won't let up—not for a second.

See, I knew this world would try to destroy my daughters. What I wasn't prepared for, what has been the most astounding, the most heartbreaking, is the number of mistruths coming from the Church.

I never expected to hear the same mouths that profess to *know* Christ say, "*You* are meant to be the hero of your own story."

I didn't think people who say they *follow* Christ would charge high fees to fill arenas with burdened women, teach from visions, work them into emotional highs, placate them in their sins, and stroke their self-esteems, only to push them out unequipped to face their adversary, who is prowling around, seeking their destruction.

I wouldn't have guessed that professing Christians—those who claim to believe it was their sin that nailed the Savior to that cross—would say, "I love Jesus,

> *How do we lead our daughters to know Christ, to follow Christ, to love Christ?*

and I cuss a little." How can we look at the cost of our redemption, and effectively laugh and say to the One True God, "Here . . . here's some more sin. Take this, too"?

There is a disconnect. We *say* we know Christ, that we want to follow Him, that we love Him, but is that what our lives are *really* saying?

So what are we to do? How do we lead our daughters to know Christ, to follow Christ, to love Christ?

First, we must make absolutely certain that *we* know Him—not our idea of who we would like Him to be, but the Jesus Christ revealed in Scripture. You see, only one true Christ exists. One Truth. If we try to change Jesus to fit our own preferences, we distort the Truth, and only the True Christ saves.

As we know Christ better, we must then choose to follow Him, leading our daughters by example. We must show them what it looks like to walk with Jesus, telling them of our convictions, the trust required to obey Him, the blessings that come when we do, and our sorrow and brokenness over our sin when we don't. Our daughters need to see us worship Christ with our words and our deeds.

So what about our love for Jesus? Here's the truth—we cannot love Christ if we do not know Him. The more we know Him, the more we will love

Him. When we love Christ, we will follow Him, and doing so will be our greatest joy.

I want my daughters to hear *these* teachings coming from the Church. I long for them to see God-fearing, God-honoring women live out a love for Christ in ways that encourage them to do the same. My girls need to witness the power of their Creator in lives powerfully changed by His Gospel and continuing to grow in His Word.

The first place this should be witnessed is in their very own home, in their very own mother. When my questions arise, when my doubts overwhelm, when my concerns seem to grow, Lord, let me look to You. Help me build a foundation of true faith that will hold. Teach me how to lead my daughters to know You, to follow You, and to love You.

This introduction to these letters is titled "Dear Daughters." The word "dear" means "regarded with deep affection, cherished, beloved, adored, precious." You see then that it is with the deepest affection for these precious girls that I write

Dear Daughters, . . .

CHAPTER ONE

Dear Daughters,

You are **oh** so special,
but you are not enough.

♥ ♥ ♥ ♥

"You are enough." You can find this rallying cry broadcast to women everywhere—from pulpits, in books, on the radio, all over social media, even on t-shirts. There is an intense effort to tell us just *how* enough we are. It's ringing out to athletes, artists, and academics, and perking the ears of the single, the married, and the parent. For the overworked, the under-appreciated, and the overwhelmed, it seems to be an anthem that we instantly respond to with a sigh of relief and a feeling of weight being lifted off our shoulders.

Maybe you've heard:

"You are enough just as you are; just be yourself."

"You are responsible for your own happiness."

"You can do anything you set your mind to."

"You can't fail at something God has called you to do."

Truth is, when we're alone in our thoughts and we are genuinely honest with ourselves, we know that this is not reality. That sigh of relief morphs into feelings of doubt in the pit of our stomachs. That weight we thought was lifted comes crashing down even heavier than before.

Insecurities multiply as worries flood our minds:

"If everyone says I'm enough, why do I feel so inadequate?"

"Why do I feel like I'm failing at everything?"

"I will never be good enough. I will never measure up."

What was intended as encouragement actually ends up leaving us drowning in disappointment, unable to keep pace on the treadmill of unrealistic expectations. Oh, the weight.

So, here's the truth. You are oh so special. *Dear, dear Daughters,* did you catch that? *You* are oh so special.

In fact, from the very beginning, God created you special—different, unique, set apart from all His other magnificent creations. And make no mistake, all His creations are completely remarkable. That is why so many of the scriptures give praise to God for His creation.

♥ ♥ ♥

O Lord, how many are Your works!
In wisdom You have made them all;
The earth is full of Your possessions. (Psalm 104:24)

The heavens are telling of the glory of God;
And their expanse is declaring the work of His hands. (Psalm 19:1)

You alone are the Lord.
You have made the heavens,
The heaven of heavens with all their host,
The earth and all that is on it,
The seas and all that is in them.
You give life to all of them

And the heavenly host bows down before You.
(Nehemiah 9:6)

Again and again, we see the Lord praised for His wisdom, understanding, and power on display in His marvelous creation. But out of all His incredible creatures, both in heaven and on the earth, you are the *only* one created in His image, fashioned by His hand, and given His breath of life. Your physical distinctions, mental abilities, emotional qualities, moral understanding, and spiritual state each contribute to what makes you completely distinguished from all other creation. In short, *you are **special***.

I think we use the word "special" so often and so carelessly it almost loses its impact. Maybe if we slow down and look at some common definitions, we will grasp it better: distinguished, superior, held in particular esteem, designed for a particular purpose, *dear*. Our flippant handling of the term, applying it to things that really aren't special, robs something from those that truly are. You're special by God's personal design, created in His very own image.

God created man in His own image, in the image of God He created him; male and female He created them. (Genesis 1:27)

So the LORD God caused a deep sleep to fall upon
the man, and he slept; then He took one of his ribs
and closed up the flesh at that place. The LORD
God fashioned into a woman the rib which He had
taken from the man, and brought her to the man.
(Genesis 2:21-22)

Look at this description:

O LORD, You have searched me and known *me*.
You know when I sit down and when I rise up;
You understand my thought from afar.
You scrutinize my path and my lying down,
And are intimately acquainted with all my ways.
Even before there is a word on my tongue,
Behold, O LORD, You know it all.
You have enclosed me behind and before,
And laid Your hand upon me.
Such knowledge is too wonderful for me;
It is *too* high, I cannot attain to it.
Where can I go from Your Spirit?
Or where can I flee from Your presence?
If I ascend to heaven, You are there;
If I make my bed in Sheol, behold, You are there.
If I take the wings of the dawn,
If I dwell in the remotest part of the sea,
Even there Your hand will lead me,
And Your right hand will lay hold of me.
If I say, "Surely the darkness will overwhelm me,
And the light around me will be night,"
Even the darkness is not dark to You,
And the night is as bright as the day.

Darkness and light are alike to *You*.
For You formed my inward parts;
You wove me in my mother's womb.
I will give thanks to You, for I am fearfully and
    wonderfully made;
Wonderful are Your works,
And my soul knows it very well.
My frame was not hidden from You,
When I was made in secret,
And skillfully wrought in the depths of the earth;
Your eyes have seen my unformed substance;
And in Your book were all written
The days that were ordained *for me*,
When as yet there was not one of them.
    (Psalm 139:1-16)

♥ ♥ ♥ ♥

How amazing! God *knows* us—intimately knows us. He knows our whereabouts, our thoughts, our actions, and each one of our days. This passage tells us God fearfully and wonderfully made us.

I'm not sure if it was God's love that propelled Him to make us special, or if it's because we're special that God loves us.

"Fearfully" means in a manner that is deserving of respect or awe. In this word choice, we see our Creator was personally involved in forming us in such a way as to leave us astonished. The Hebrew word for "wonderfully" means God made us to be distinct, separated, marked for a particular purpose, distinguished, and wonderful. Literally, He made us special—in *every* meaning of the word.

A popular kids' series used to end every show with: "God made you special, and He loves you very much."[1] How beautiful is this truth? I'm not sure if it was God's love that propelled Him to make us special, or if it's because we're special that God loves us. But this truth remains—the Lord loves you. He loves you unconditionally, and He has from the beginning of time, before your days had even begun. In His Word, He tells us:

We love, because He first loved us. (1 John 4:19)

Are not five sparrows sold for two cents? *Yet* not one of them is forgotten before God. Indeed, the very hairs of your head are all numbered. Do not fear; you are more valuable than many sparrows. (Luke 12:6-7)

But God demonstrates His own love toward us, in that while we were yet sinners, Christ died for us. (Romans 5:8)

For God so loved the world, that He gave His only begotten Son, that whoever believes in Him shall not perish, but have eternal life. (John 3:16)

> He loves us without provocation, without condition, and without limits. We're special to Him. We're dear to Him so cherished, so treasured, so precious that He died for us.

It is abundantly clear that God loves us. He loves us without provocation, without condition, and without limits. We're special to Him. We're *dear* to Him—so cherished, so treasured, so precious that He died for us. If you ever wonder about your worth, lift your eyes to the Lamb of God who paid your ransom in full that day. Through His willing submission to a terrible death on the cross of Calvary as the sacrifice for our sins, the Lord Jesus Christ showed us just how valuable we are to Him. Our value, our worth was fixed at that moment. It can never be taken away. It is forever set at the cross. What astounding love the Father has lavished on us. How clear it is. You are oh so special.

But you are not enough.

That's why when we're lying in our beds at night and everything is quiet and dark, we're overwhelmed with lists and doubts and fears. Trying to measure ourselves against some impossible standard on social media or reality television, we have bought into the lie that our answer exists somewhere inside ourselves.

"If I could just get up earlier, stay up later, work harder, study longer, or move faster, I could be enough."

"Maybe I could give more, be stronger, have more positive thoughts, really try to stay in the moment, or set bigger goals. Then I could be enough."

We try and we try. We work harder, faster, and longer, but we still can't get it all done. I believe we're really longing for relief, freedom, peace, and rest. The problem is, we've been looking at the wrong source. The world says the answer is within you, and sadly, it seems many within the Church have believed this lie. Anytime we look within ourselves for the solutions to our problems, for strength, endurance, peace, or freedom, we're going to come up short. The wreckage can be found all around us. Anxiety, depression, stress, and brokenness mark our day. And it's nothing new; it's all throughout Scripture.

There is a way *which* seems right to a man,
But its end is the way of death. (Proverbs 16:25)

He who trusts in his own heart is a fool,
But he who walks wisely will be delivered.
(Proverbs 28:26)

Trust in the Lord with all your heart
And do not lean on your own understanding.
(Proverbs 3:5)

The Bible is clear. The answer is *not* within you. It never was. You are not enough. All your strength, all your resolve, all your endurance will never bring you the peace or the freedom you're looking for. The reality is you're inadequate, unable to measure up to the standard that has been set. That standard *isn't* found on social media or reality television. It was set by our Creator. In Romans, we read that everybody has fallen short of it. Everybody.

The standard is to "LOVE THE LORD YOUR GOD WITH ALL YOUR HEART, AND WITH ALL YOUR SOUL, AND WITH ALL YOUR MIND" (Matthew 22:37). Our love is shown in our obedience. 1 John 5:3 says, "For this is the love of God, that we keep His commandments; and His commandments are not burdensome." Those who trust in the Lord will love and obey Him.

Ever since the Garden, our problem has been the same—we don't really trust in the Lord. Our hearts are divided, and we disobey Him. We have no peace because we have no peace with our Creator. We have no freedom because we're bound in our chains of sin and death. No amount of personal strength or good effort can free us from them, "but thanks be to God, who gives us the victory through our Lord Jesus Christ" (1 Corinthians 15:57).

See, you and I *need* a Savior. Our *only* hope is in a Savior, and that is exactly what we have in God who became flesh, lived a sinless life, died in our place, paid our ransom in full, and rose victoriously from the dead. When we humble ourselves, recognizing that we are not enough, and we trust in the One who is, the Bible says that "having been justified by faith, we have peace with God through our Lord Jesus Christ" (Romans 5:1). By confessing our defeat in our own sin, we are given victory through Christ. By admitting our sinful shortcomings, we're pulled from the wreckage of our own making by our sinless Savior.

Our answer is in Him. Our strength is in Him. Our peace is in Him. Our hope is in Him. You are not enough. Oh, but He is.

Therefore, He is able also to save forever those who draw near to God through Him, since He always lives to make intercession for them. (Hebrews 7:25)

So what about your day-to-day life when doubts start to creep in amid the busyness, and you feel like you're back on the treadmill of unrealistic expectations? Then, *dear Daughters*, remember this: God, Himself, who is able to raise Jesus from the dead, has given you His Word, and He is able to make you adequate—to make you enough, and to equip you for everything He has called you to do for His glory. So, when you start to feel inadequate, and the fears and doubts creep in, go to His Word. The answer lies only in Him. He will teach you, correct you, encourage you, and equip you to do His will.

Now the God of peace, who brought up from the dead the great Shepherd of the sheep through the blood of the eternal covenant, *even* Jesus our Lord, equip you in every good thing to do His will, working in us that which is pleasing in His sight, through Jesus Christ, to whom *be* the glory forever and ever. Amen. (Hebrews 13:20-21)

All Scripture is inspired by God and profitable for teaching, for reproof, for correction, for training in righteousness; so that the man of God may be adequate, equipped for every good work. (2 Timothy 3:16-17)

Dear Daughters, there is good news in realizing you're not enough. For it's in looking to Jesus—the only One who is—that you will find true relief, real freedom, unfathomable peace, and everlasting rest.

CHAPTER TWO

Dear Daughters,

Biblical Christianity doesn't mean you're less than a man in God's plan.

"**I** can't ever do what you do," a little girl with tears in her eyes told her pastor daddy one night. She had come to the point in her life when she started to understand that God made men and women different, assigning them unique roles. For a daddy's girl who had long dreamed of being just like her dad, this realization was heartbreaking. Seeing his daughter hurting didn't set easy with her father, either, and he lovingly tried to guide her to grow in the knowledge of God's truth.

The truth he shared, the truth we all need to know is this: biblical Christianity doesn't mean you're less than a man in God's plan. So, then why do we think that it does? Why are lots of women and men convinced that women are somehow inferior to men in God's eyes or even by His design? I'm afraid that the answer may lie in this: Christianity has been and continues to be twisted to oppress women—to put them down simply because they were born female.

It started fairly early in church history with men who were hailed as some of the first Christian theologians and church influencers.

God maintained the order of each sex by dividing the business of human life into two parts and assigned the more necessary and beneficial aspects to the man and the less important, inferior matters to the woman. —John Chrysostom[2]

What is the difference whether it is in a wife or a mother, it is still Eve the temptress that we must beware of in any woman . . . I fail to see what use woman can be to man, if one excludes the function of bearing children. —Saint Augustine of Hippo[3]

Woman was merely man's helpmate, a function which pertains to her alone. She is not the image of God but as far as man is concerned, he is by himself the image of God. —Saint Augustine of Hippo[4]

Let the woman be satisfied with her state of subjection, and not take it amiss that she is made inferior to the more distinguished sex. —John Calvin[5]

Modern teachers of Christianity sometimes promote these same flawed conclusions. For example, the account of Adam and Eve is improperly interpreted or applied to support the teaching that women are inferior to men. It's also said that the apostle Paul held a low view of women.[6] Misinterpretations of his letters are used as a license to suppress women into complete silence, claiming they are not permitted to read Scriptures or even pray in the church. Other distorted teachings claim that submission would only ever be required of those who are less than or secondary.

When you read these hurtful and harmful lies written by people claiming the name of Christ, yet insulting and demeaning half of His created mankind, it's hard not to take offense. It's also plain to see why many women have waged an all-out war against these ideas in the name of feminism, many of whom have left Christianity altogether. Even the smallest look into this serious and age-old debate will leave you convinced that people on all sides have been hurt and remain divided by discussions about gender.

> The problem is that what has been taught as a "Christian" worldview is not a biblical worldview.

The problem is that what has been taught as a "Christian" worldview is not a *biblical* worldview.

That is not our God. That is not His Word.

As believers and as students of God's Word, we must be careful in our response to gender issues. Our response is triggered by our beliefs. If we want to be correct in our beliefs, we cannot take anyone's word for what those beliefs should be. We must look to see what God, Himself, has said about His creation of women, His view of women, and His plan for women.

God's Creation of Women

In the book of Genesis, we read about God's creation of the first man, Adam. As God looks at the man, He sees he is alone and needs a suitable helper or helpmeet. The words for this in Hebrew are *ezer kenegdo*, which carries the meaning of a corresponding strength, a help that is facing, or an equal opposite. Think of it like a right leg and a left leg or two halves of the same circle. Of all the creatures the Lord made, none of them were found to be Adam's *ezer kenegdo*. So, God put Adam to sleep, took out one of his ribs, and fashioned it into a woman—a strength that corresponds to man.

God is clear: He created mankind in His image—male *and* female. He walked with them both, blessed them both, gave them both the command to be fruitful and multiply, to fill the earth and to rule over it. According to the Bible, when God created the first man and woman, it's apparent they were on equal footing before Him by His design.

Jesus' View of Women

To see how God views women, I think it best to look to how Jesus, the perfect representation—the exact image—of God on Earth treated and interacted with them. Understanding the cultural context into which Jesus was born will help us to truly grasp God's considerations of the women He created. Jesus was born a Jew into the Roman culture during a time when women of both cultures were severely oppressed.

Roman women were not allowed to be involved in politics, were always considered dependents of the oldest male of their families, were not counted as legal guardians of their own children, and were generally considered an essential inconvenience.

Jewish women were held in high esteem, in theory, but the practice by which they were treated said otherwise. They had no legal status and were forbidden from testifying in court, along with minors, Gentiles, and other "undesirables," due to the "levity and boldness of their sex."[7] Respectable Jewish women were not to go to the marketplace unless under heavy duress, and even then, had to be heavily veiled and refrain from conversing with men.

Jewish rabbis considered women exempt from the command to learn the Law of Moses, teaching, "It is foolishness to teach the Torah to your daughter,"[8] and causing many women to be illiterate. Though there was no such court described in the instructions for building the Temple, by Jesus' day, women were only permitted to the confines of the Women's Court and were kept separate from men, not even allowed to pray publicly.[9] Jewish law allowed only the man to begin the divorce process, and it allowed for divorce for the smallest of reasons, such as a burned meal.

It was into this world, where women were considered second-rate, that our God condescended. And in the midst of these wounded women, our Savior traveled, taught, and ministered.

Contrary to the teachings of self-serving rabbis, Jesus commended one of His closest friends, Mary, for sitting at His feet and learning from Him. You see, two women, Mary and her sister Martha, were some of Jesus' *dearest* friends.

In fact, Jesus had a core of faithful women who traveled with Him throughout His ministry, some of whom supported His cause financially. He gladly conversed, taught, and ministered to women and men, both together in groups and as individuals. Despite the fact that even His disciples "were amazed that He had been speaking with a woman" (John 4:27), Jesus took His opportunity to tell the woman at the well, caught in her sin, that He was the Messiah. Can you imagine being a woman in this society—a Samaritan woman, no less—and having a Jewish man speak to you? The most amazing thing about this account is that Jesus didn't just speak to her. He pinpointed her sin and expressed her need for a Savior. He told her about the gift of God, taught her about living water and eternal life, and affirmed that she was speaking with the very Savior she needed. What astounding love He must have had for this woman.

According to Scripture, a group of women remained faithful to Christ through the entire Crucifixion, and they were there for His burial. Women were the first to see Jesus resurrected. It was a woman, Mary Magdalene—not even permitted by Jewish law to testify in court—who was told by

Jesus to be the one to testify to His disciples that He was no longer dead.

Women were present with Jesus, following, listening, learning, blessing, serving, supporting, announcing, anointing, and believing Him. In His many recorded interactions with women, Jesus never put them down, never humiliated, never disparaged, or condemned them. Mothers and daughters, single and married, sick and well, grieving and rejoicing, Jews and foreigners, women of high standing and women of ill-repute—Jesus held each one *dear*.

God's View of Women in His Word

God's view of women is also made clear in His Word, as He gives accounts of His interactions with them, and as He gives wisdom and direction for Christian life and practice. By a deeper look at just a few verses and the Bible as a whole, we can be sure that God values women. Throughout the Scriptures, women were able to go directly to God in prayer and were not seen as spiritually inferior to men. Some women were prophetesses, some served as judges, and some took vows of sanctification in service to the Lord.

In Proverbs, God's Word says, "He who finds a wife finds a good thing And obtains favor from the LORD," (Prov. 18:22) and "House and wealth are an inheritance from fathers, But a prudent" (or wise) "wife is from the LORD" (Prov.19:14). Undoubtedly, you would be hard-pressed to find a more glowing commendation of any person than the woman described in Proverbs 31.

In 1 Peter, men are commanded to show honor to or to value their wives as fellow heirs to the grace and loveliness of life. In Ephesians, husbands are told to love their wives as they love themselves, giving sacrificially for them, nourishing and cherishing them, and being completely unified with them. These instructions for men stood in shocking contrast to the culture and were established to set followers of Christ apart from the world.

In God's Word, we see accounts of women who served alongside men in ministry, teaching, and evangelism. They were present in the gatherings of the early Church, and they were not prohibited from praying or worshiping. Throughout Scripture, **including** the letters from Paul, women were praised and thanked for their great faith, hard work, service to the Lord, sacrifice, and help to the cause. God sends His angels, His messengers, to speak directly to women and includes women in the most miraculous ways in His perfect plan of redemption.

> *Mothers and daughters, single and married, sick and well, grieving and rejoicing, Jews, and foreigners, women of high standing and women of ill-repute Jesus held each one dear.*

In stark contrast to the view that society held, and unlike any other religious group, our God holds women in high esteem. Jesus, God in flesh, was radical in His love for them, and He showcased that love as He taught, blessed, fed, healed, discipled, commissioned, and forgave women. The greatest demonstration of His love for women was at the cross where He made the way for their salvation. In Galatians 3:28-29, we read that for any who placed their faith in Christ Jesus, "there is neither male nor female; for you are all one in Christ Jesus . . . heirs according to promise."

But, what about submission?

Some may ask about the Bible's call for submission. Isn't that where we find unreasonable and oppressive restrictions limiting what women can do for God's kingdom? Doesn't submission mean someone is less than or weaker than someone else? In Ephesians 5, there is a Biblical command for women to submit to their husbands. The book of 1 Peter, talking about a submissive wife, actually calls her "someone weaker." Do these verses mean, as some have supposed, that women are second-rate? Be sure, many of the harmful misperceptions and demeaning attitudes endured by women have originated from a poor, even sinful application of Biblical submission.

To understand Biblical submission, we first need a definition of what submission actually is and what it is not. Submission is voluntarily yielding oneself to another, making oneself subject to, or the act of deferring to. It has nothing to do with worth, value, or potential. And submission cannot be forced on someone. It is a voluntary act. The Biblical call to submit is not based on superiority or inferiority, but rather out of reverence for God and trust in His goodness, wisdom, and faithfulness. Get that—it is not done in inferiority, but in trust and reverence for God!

It is important to understand the reference to "someone weaker" in 1 Peter 3:7 is addressing only physical stature—not intellectual, emotional, moral, or spiritual strength. Submission, in practice, is not done by a weak person, but rather a resolved person. It is actually a great act of strong faith. It is carried out by only the strongest of people.

A clear understanding of perfect Biblical submission is found in looking to Christ. Jesus is fully God. Scripture tells us He and the Father are one, are equal. Jesus—fully God—voluntarily, willingly (remember the definition) submitted Himself to the will of the Father. In doing so, He was not weak, inferior, or less than God. In fact, because of this, the Bible says He is exalted above everyone else.

So, you see, submission is not demeaning, not devaluing, not a sign of weakness. It requires a deep and true knowledge of God. It shows a deep trust and obedience in God. And the greatest thing—it heaps great, great glory on God! He is worthy!

God's Plan for Women

The Bible absolutely teaches that men and women are different. It is clear they have different roles in life, in the family, and in the church. But when those within the church teach that women are less valuable, less worthy of contributing to the cause of Christ than men simply based on our gender, they are falling into Satan's destructive plan. The result of this teaching is pain, division, oppression, and a distortion of the Gospel of Jesus Christ. That was never God's plan. That is not our God. That is not His Word.

So, what is God's plan for women? While God has created men and women different, while He has given us different roles, and while submission is part of His called-for order, God's plan for women is to equally, fully glorify God. God receives the most glory whenever a life is restored to a right relationship with Him that then points other people to a right relationship with Him. He is most glorified in a life turned over to Him, learning, growing, obeying, serving, ministering, giving, worshiping, and testifying. The Lord gifts believers—all believers—differently. The point of doing this is that believers would complement one another in His service and for His cause.

However, in the Lord, neither is woman independent of man, nor is man independent of woman. For as the woman originates from the man, so also the man *has his birth* through the woman; and all things originate from God. (1 Corinthians 11:11-12)

Now there are varieties of gifts, but the same Spirit. And there are varieties of ministries, and the same Lord. There are varieties of effects, but the same God who works all things in all *persons*. But to each one is given the manifestation of the Spirit for the common good. (1 Corinthians 12:4-7)

The Creator God's plan is that men and women would serve each other and that they would serve *with* each other—each complementing the other to God's glory. *Ezer Kenegdo*. Men, as a gender, are better when strengthened by their equal and opposite counterpart: women. The Lord, in His infinite wisdom, by His great power, and in His unmeasurable love, created women. His plan for them is to be a strength, a complement that meets men where they are. His plan for them is to use the gifts He has given them, offering their lives as living and holy sacrifices, which is their spiritual act of worship (Romans 12:1). His plan is for them to bring Him glory.

> The Lord, in His infinite wisdom, by His great power, and in His unmeasurable love, created women.

In the end, that little girl heard this truth: she may end up leading more people to Christ than any pastor ever does. She, like every other female ever created, has the potential to bring God every bit as much glory and honor as any man. *Dear Daughters,* the same is true of *you*. Biblical Christianity does not mean you're less than a man in God's plan. Your life given over to the Lord in complete surrender, is as pleasing and as glorifying as any other life could ever be.

CHAPTER THREE

Dear Daughters,

You will need direction. God's Word is His biggest blessing to you.

ome people in this world, like my brother, are naturally capable of finding their way around. Even as a child, he just *knew* the fastest, most efficient, sometimes back-road route to get just about anywhere. It just comes so easily to him. And, then, there are people like me. I can get turned around in a shopping center parking lot and need the assistance of Siri just to get me out. When people try to use words like "north" or "east," my eyes grow wide, and my heart beats a little faster in panic. Trust me, I am *not* the one you want to ride shotgun. I need direction.

In this crazy hard, yet beautiful life, the same is true for all people. We need direction. We need answers. Every day, we face a multitude of questions. Some are profound, and others seemingly insignificant. Yet each one requires an answer from us. Paper or plastic? Stay or go? Left or right? Chocolate or vanilla? Right or wrong? Each one of us also has a variety of places to look for the answers we need. Some look to popular culture or to their friends, peers, or family members. Some look to the experts, the authorities, or the professionals. Some will look back at history to seek answers to today's questions. Still others will be self-directed, looking to be led by their own feelings, personal desires, or emotions.

The sum of our lives will be made up of the answers to the questions we face. The success of that sum will be determined by the strength of our answers, and the strength of our answers depends upon the source of those answers.

How blessed is the man who does not walk in the
    counsel of the wicked,
Nor stand in the path of sinners,
Nor sit in the seat of scoffers!
But his delight is in the law of the LORD,
And in His law he meditates day and night.
He will be like a tree *firmly* planted by streams of water,
Which yields its fruit in its season
And its leaf does not wither;
And in whatever he does he prospers. (Psalm 1:1-3)

Thus says the LORD,
"Cursed is the man who trusts in mankind
And makes flesh his strength,
And whose heart turns away from the LORD.
"For he will be like a bush in the desert
And will not see when prosperity comes,
But will live in stony wastes in the wilderness,
A land of salt without inhabitant.
"Blessed is the man who trusts in the LORD
And whose trust is the LORD.
"For he will be like a tree planted by the water,
That extends its roots by a stream
And will not fear when the heat comes;
But its leaves will be green,
And it will not be anxious in a year of drought
Nor cease to yield fruit." (Jeremiah 17:5-8)

♥ ♥ ♥♥

Dear Daughters, God knew you would need direction. Thankfully, we have a Creator who is all-knowing, completely wise, and infinitely gracious. He gives us His Word and it's His greatest blessing to us.

Be Sure: God's Word is the Truth

"What is truth?"

Two thousand years ago, a Roman governor posed this question as a King stood on trial before him, testifying to the truth. Mankind has always sought a truth to provide structure, order, and meaning to life. Ancient philosophers like Plato, Aristotle, and Socrates loved and searched for knowledge, asking questions about reality, truth, and the nature and meaning of existence. Nietzsche, Marx, and Thoreau sought intellectual enlightenment and had a major impact on the public, politics, and popular culture. In recent years, philosophy has become a profession, causing an explosion of philosophy majors in universities and a huge increase in the volume of published works. Today, despite thousands of years of deep thinkers and theorists, it seems people are *still* searching for truth.

So, what is truth? It is that which is real, genuine, authentic, and sincere. Truth is a set of facts that are reality. It is actuality. "In God's Word, truth refers to that which is revealed, unconcealed, made known, or manifest. Truth is, well . . . true. It's all true. It's completely true. It's exclusively true.

An idea that looks to be picking up speed, especially in Christian circles, is that there can be more than one truth. This is pluralism, or the holding of two or more positions at the same time. Pluralism is the idea that there is plenty of room for every idea. Jump on the comments of just about any social media post and you'll likely see people use phrases such as, "She's just sharing her truth," or "Well, that's his truth," or "Speak your truth." Here's the thing—her truth, his truth, your truth, and my truth do not exist. There is only **the** truth.

Truth, by its definition, means that all else is *not* the truth—it is false. Truth, by its very nature, is exclusive. It's distinct and separate from anything else. It's either true or it's not. Shades of truth, partial truths, and multiple truths do not exist.

On the night of the Last Supper, in His High Priestly Prayer, Jesus prayed for those who would make up the Church following His crucifixion and resurrection. He knew about the incredible persecution they would face. He also knew about all the lies—blatant and subtle—that would be spread, seeking to destroy His Church. In the face of all of this, Jesus prayed for them to have the knowledge of Him, as He had been manifested or made known to them. The Messiah then prayed for their unity, and for them to be set apart in the truth.

Sanctify them in the truth; Your word is truth. (John 17:17)

Jesus, the Truth, testified to the truth and prayed for believers to be unified in the truth. He said God's Word is truth. And He said the purpose for it—the reason for the truth, the revealed, the genuine—is so the world would *know* God.

All of mankind—from professional philosophers to young fathers on their tractors to little girls lying in their beds at night—all people are looking for the truth. You can have it. Christ, Himself, prayed for it. We find it in God's Word. The one *true* God is revealed to us that we might *know* Him.

Be Sure: God's Word Will Stand

There's an old adage that goes, "It has stood the test of time." Today, it seems not much can meet that standard. Firmly held ideas, once embraced as bedrock truths, have eroded over time. If you were to travel to Paris and enter the Library of the Louvre, you would see three and a half miles of books about science. Almost all of them are now considered obsolete. A once-accepted medical theory called "humorism" said having too much or too little of certain bodily fluids was to blame for all health issues and even changes in temperament. This belief led to medical practices such as bloodletting. In 1799, George Washington had more than half his blood withdrawn because he was sick with a throat infection. He died within a few days.[10]

And He said the purpose for it the reason for the truth, the revealed, the genuine is so the world would know God.

Now almost laughable, by 1964, trying to combat a growing concern about a link between cigarette smoking and health issues, the R.J. Reynolds Tobacco Company ran their new campaign slogan: "More doctors smoke Camels than any other cigarette."[11] Other companies ran similar ads, some actually trying to claim health benefits customers would receive by using their brands. The CEO for Philip Morris, the maker of Marlboro, said, "It's true that babies born from women who smoke are smaller, but they are just as healthy as the babies born to women who do not smoke. Some women would prefer having smaller babies."[12]

For another example, at the end of the 18th century, the age of the earth was estimated to be 75,000 years old, then hundreds of millions of years old at the end of the 19th century, and 4.5 billion years old at the end of the 20th century.[13]

We exist in a world that has trained us to believe that truth changes. We live in a culture of relativism, where the truth is said to be relative to the individual or group holding to it. People believe that because of the limited nature of the mind and the conditions of knowledge, truth is dependent on the person or situation. In today's world, it is supposed that truth must be shaped, instead of recognized. As a result, the perception is there is no concrete truth—it's all relative.

But God says otherwise:

The grass withers, the flower fades,
But the word of our God stands forever. (Isaiah 40:8)

Forever, O LORD,
Your word is settled in heaven. (Psalm 119:89)

. . . for you have been born again not of seed which is perishable but imperishable, *that is*, through the living and enduring word of God. (1 Peter 1:23)

That's the thing about *the* truth—it's unchanging. If it shifted based on circumstances or people or the passage of time or *any* other factor, it could not, by definition, be true.

In today's culture, tolerance, not truth, is esteemed as the greatest virtue. This idea of relativism has so captured our minds that anyone who even hints at the truth, saying absolutes exist and they are unchanging, is labeled intolerant. It has even crept into the Church, where you can hear people make the following claims when discussing Scripture: "Well, that's not what that verse means *to me,*" or "That's just *your* interpretation."

If God's Word is truth—*The Truth*—and if He desires that we would be unified in the truth, and if the truth is unchanging, then that means we can know what a passage *means*, and we can hold the correct interpretation. It is not to be subjectively determined or created by us; it is to be discovered or made known to us.

But when He, the Spirit of truth, comes, He will guide you into all the truth. (John 16:13)

So Jesus was saying to those Jews who had believed Him, "If you continue in My word, *then* you are truly disciples of Mine; and you will know the truth, and the truth will make you free." (John 8:31-32)

As disciples of Christ, we are to continue learning and growing in His word. While we look to His guidance to bring us to all truth, we keep a humble spirit and ask for the Lord to grant us wisdom. We can do this in great confidence, knowing that it's His desire for us to know the truth and that the truth is not shifting. God's Word is truth, and God's Word will stand.

Be Sure: God's Word Is Enough

Have you ever wished God would just speak to you—like really speak to you? Well then, take hope. God *has* spoken. He has spoken through His prophets and through His Son, and His words are recorded for us in Scripture. Moreover, what God has said is the truth, which means it's unchanging, absolute, unconcealed, and sufficient.

All Scripture is inspired by God and profitable for teaching, for reproof, for correction, for training in righteousness; so that the man of God may be adequate, equipped for every good work. (2 Timothy 3:16-17)

But know this first of all, that no prophecy of Scripture is *a matter* of one's own interpretation, for no prophecy was ever made by an act of human will, but men moved by the Holy Spirit spoke from God. (2 Peter 1:20-21)

God, after He spoke long ago to the fathers in the prophets in many portions and in many ways, in these last days has spoken to us in His Son, whom He appointed heir of all things, through whom also He made the world. (Hebrews 1:1-2)

So what does this mean? It means we do not need the traditions of men, an expert opinion, a vision, or someone's experiences. We don't need a new word, a fresh word, or a deeper word, because we have *the* Word. What we do need is to be completely convinced that God's Word is enough for us.

Grace and peace be multiplied to you in the knowledge of God and of Jesus our Lord; seeing that His divine power has granted to us everything pertaining to life and godliness, through the true knowledge of Him who called us by His own glory and excellence. (2 Peter 1:2-3)

You see, we have the knowledge of God by His revelation through Jesus Christ. In His Word, we have everything we need for matters of faith *and* life. The Bible is not something that we can compartmentalize, selling it short as a book that speaks only to issues of religion. The Bible is a supernatural, powerful, and practical guide for *all* areas of life. It is when we truly see that

We don't need a new word, a fresh word, or a deeper word, because we have the Word. What we do need is to be completely convinced that God's Word is enough for us.

God's Word is sufficient that we will be drawn deeper into the study of it, and there discover the truth and be "equipped for every good work."

> How firm a foundation, ye saints
> of the Lord,
> is laid for your faith in His excellent Word!
> What more can He say than to
> you He hath said,
> who unto the Savior for refuge
> have fled?[14]

Be Sure: God's Word Will Direct Us

Because God's Word is the truth from the Creator Himself, because we can trust that it will stand, and because we know that it's enough, we can confidently turn to God's Word as the source of direction in our lives. Listen to these words of Christ:

Therefore everyone who hears these words of Mine and acts on them, may be compared to a wise man who built his house on the rock. And the rain fell, and the floods came, and the winds blew and slammed against that house; and *yet* it did not fall, for it had been founded on the rock. Everyone who hears these words of Mine and does not act on them, will be like a foolish man who built his house on the sand. The rain fell, and the floods came, and the winds blew and slammed against that house; and it fell—and great was its fall. (Matthew 7:24-27)

His words are the rock. These words of His are a firm foundation. We can trust the Bible to safely lead us in all areas of our lives. God, in His great grace, has given us direction for how to speak, how to study, and how to spend. From practical wisdom on parenting to proven insight for marriages, the Lord wants to give you wisdom.

But if any of you lacks wisdom, let him ask of God, who gives to all generously and without reproach, and it will be given to him. (James 1:5)

When you wonder: What about giving? What about gossip? What about grace? The answers are there. How should I dress? What should I watch? How should I work? His guidance is there. He tells us what to embrace and what to avoid. He speaks to health, wealth, and happiness. He speaks to big matters and small matters, and every time He speaks, He uncovers truth for those who seek it.

God, in His infinite knowledge, knew we would need direction. And in His infinite grace, He gave

My own life changed when I realized that the Bible is not a book of dead words that only applied to an irrelevant culture that has long since disappeared. His words are not dead, not outdated, not weak.

us exactly what we need in His Word. It's not *another* way to live, and it's not a *good* way to live; it is the absolute *best* way to live. We have instructions from the Creator Himself—the One who loves us, who holds us *dear*, and who wants what is best for us.

My own life changed when I realized that the Bible is not a book of dead words that only applied to an irrelevant culture that has long since disappeared. His words are not dead, not outdated, not weak. At one time in my life I was actually afraid to talk about certain topics for fear that I would somehow prove the Bible to be outdated. When I think back on those days, I can't help but laugh at myself. I also can't help but thank God for His mercy and grace in opening my eyes to the truth. His words are not dead, not outdated, not weak.

For the word of God is living and active and sharper than any two-edged sword, and piercing as far as the division of soul and spirit, of both joints and marrow, and able to judge the thoughts and intentions of the heart. (Hebrews 4:12)

Dear Daughters, as you move through these days that make up your lives, my prayer for you is that you would look to God's words and hear Him as He speaks through them to you, for you. For it's in those moments that you will come away awe-struck, saying, "It's like God was speaking just to me." You will need direction. God's Word is His biggest blessing to you.

CHAPTER FOUR

Dear Daughters,

*Success doesn't look
like what you think.
Only chase what matters.*

*T*oday, an estimated 184,000 baby girls[15] will draw their first breath and begin to live out the span of their lives. On average, they will be afforded 648,684 hours, or 27,028 days, or 3,848 weeks, or 74 years.[16] Each one will have only a certain number of hours to spend on this earth. As these hours go by, sometimes dragging, sometimes racing, all of us will be chasing something. Most people will spend those hours chasing success. Merriam-Webster defines success as "a measure of succeeding; a favorable outcome; the attainment of wealth, favor, or eminence."

Looking around today, it's not difficult to determine what the world counts as success. People chase jobs they can call fulfilling, education to get better jobs, and money—always more money. We want nicer houses, newer cars, and the latest technology. We want lives that look great on social media, complete with matching outfits. Our desire for popularity and approval keeps us coming back to see how many likes we can generate post by post.

As a whole, we live in the most prosperous, most advanced, most advantageous time in our nation's history. Even some of the poorest households have an abundance of comforts that previous generations could never have dreamed of—not just air conditioning, washers and dryers, and other appliances, but multiple televisions, multiple smartphones, internet access, video game systems, and on-demand movies. Our communities connect us to entertainment, shopping, and dining, and most homes have more than one vehicle to drive us to these luxuries. This is our normal.

Yet even surrounded by all of this extravagance and ease, people aren't satisfied. Seventy percent of the working people in the U.S. refer to themselves as "unhappy."[17] Our culture, as a whole, describes itself as unfulfilled, bored, and even stuck. Prescriptions for anti-depressants have increased by more than 400% since 1988,[18] with women being 2.5 times more likely to take them than men.[19] Suicide rates are steadily increasing, as well, and it's currently the 10th leading cause of death.[20] Chasing after success doesn't seem to be paying off.

Most of this disillusionment, if not all of it, can be attributed to a flawed view of success. People are devoting their time and energy—the span of their lives—to chase things that ultimately cannot produce fulfillment or satisfaction. They are running and striving and competing to achieve or to acquire something, only to find the pursuit empty and the result hollow. *Dear Daughters,* hear me. Success doesn't look like what you think. Only chase what matters.

Nothing New Under the Sun

In the Bible, King Solomon is known for two things: his tremendous wisdom and his wealth that exceeded that of all the kings of the earth. It's estimated that his net worth today would be around $2.2 trillion. Here's how Solomon describes his achievements:

I enlarged my works: I built houses for myself, I planted vineyards for myself; I made gardens and parks for myself and I planted in them all kinds of fruit trees; I made ponds of water for myself from which to irrigate a forest of growing trees. I bought male and female slaves and I had homeborn slaves. Also I possessed flocks and herds larger than all who preceded me in Jerusalem. Also, I collected for myself silver and gold and the treasure of kings and provinces. I provided for myself male and female singers and the pleasures of men—many concubines. Then I became great and increased more than all who preceded me in Jerusalem. My wisdom also stood by me. All that my eyes desired I did not refuse them. I did not withhold my heart from any pleasure, for my heart was pleased because of all my labor and this was my reward for all my labor. (Ecclesiastes 2:4-10)

If you could ever look at a man and say, "This guy actually pulled it off. He was successful," you could say that about Solomon. And if we only read this section of verses, we might be convinced he was pleased with how it all turned out for him. But, when we keep reading, we see something very different.

Thus I considered all my activities which my hands had done and the labor which I had exerted, and behold all was vanity and striving after wind and there was no profit under the sun. (Ecclesiastes 2:11)

As Solomon looked back on all his achievements, he said it was all vanity—empty, proud, unsatisfactory self-worship. Though he seems to have succeeded by the world's standards, he says that all the education, all the pleasure, and all the wealth amounted to nothing.

Jesus had this to say:

For what will it profit a man if he gains the whole world and forfeits his soul? (Matthew 16:26)

If the world's ideas of success are flawed, then what is true success? What should we strive for? How can we avoid coming to the end of our lives and finding we have chased after the wind? To find the answer, we must look to the truth of God's Word.

Do not store up for yourselves treasures on earth, where moth and rust destroy, and where thieves break in and steal. But store up for yourselves treasures in heaven, where neither moth nor rust destroys, and where thieves do not break in or steal; for where your treasure is, there your heart will be also. (Matthew 6:19-21)

Jesus tells us in these verses not to store up, gather, accumulate, or heap up treasures on earth. He says that anything we might manage to pile up on earth can be trashed or taken away from us. It will only be temporary; it won't last. Instead, He directs us to store up treasures in heaven. These are eternal blessings that God promises to those who have trusted in Christ for their salvation.

What is done out of a love for Christ, what is carried out by His Spirit, what is motivated by a longing to bring Him glory—these things will be rewarded by our good and generous God. These treasures will be far, *far* better than anything we might ever receive on this earth. And these treasures cannot ever be destroyed or taken from us. They are everlasting. We see here that all of it, whether worldly or heavenly, temporary or eternal, is determined by and reveals our heart. As we look to see what success truly is, we must ask ourselves, "Where is my heart?"

What is done out of a love for Christ, what is carried out by His Spirit, what is motivated by a longing to bring Him glory—these things will be rewarded by our good and generous God.

Throughout the Old and New Testaments, God's definition of success is consistent. Love God, seek Him, serve Him, declare His praises, and go and tell others about Him. Make the most of your time. You won't get these hours back.

Solomon, in all his wisdom, and with his realization that all the worldly success amounted to nothing, said this:

The conclusion, when all has been heard, *is*: fear God and keep His commandments, because this *applies to* every person. For God will bring every act to judgment, everything which is hidden, whether it is good or evil. (Ecclesiastes 12:13–14)

A missionary named C.T. Studd wrote this incredibly profound poem:[21]

Two little lines I heard one day,
Traveling along life's busy way;
Bringing conviction to my heart,
And from my mind would not depart;
Only one life, 'twill soon be past,
Only what's done for Christ will last.

Only one life, yes only one,
Soon will its fleeting hours be done;
Then, in "that day" my Lord to meet,
And stand before His Judgement seat;
Only one life, 'twill soon be past,
Only what's done for Christ will last.

Only one life, the still small voice,
Gently pleads for a better choice
Bidding me selfish aims to leave,
And to God's holy will to cleave;
Only one life, 'twill soon be past,
Only what's done for Christ will last.

Only one life, a few brief years,
Each with its burdens, hopes, and fears;
Each with its clays I must fulfill,
living for self or in His will;
Only one life, 'twill soon be past,
Only what's done for Christ will last.

When this bright world would tempt me sore,
When Satan would a victory score;
When self would seek to have its way,

Then help me Lord with joy to
say;
Only one life, 'twill soon be past,
Only what's done for Christ will
last.

Give me Father, a purpose
deep,
In joy or sorrow Thy word to
keep;
Faithful and true what e'er the
strife,
Pleasing Thee in my daily life;
Only one life, 'twill soon be past,
Only what's done for Christ
will last.

*Love God, seek Him,
serve Him, declare
His praises, and go
and tell others about
Him. Make the
most of your time,
You won't get
these hours back.*

Oh let my love with fervor burn,
And from the world now let me turn;
Living for Thee, and Thee alone,
Bringing Thee pleasure on Thy throne;
Only one life, 'twill soon be past,
Only what's done for Christ will last.

Only one life, yes only one,
Now let me say, "Thy will be done";
And when at last I'll hear the call,
I know I'll say "'twas worth it all";
Only one life, 'twill soon be past,
Only what's done for Christ will last.

—extra stanza—
Only one life, 'twill soon be past,
Only what's done for Christ will last.
And when I am dying, how happy I'll be,
If the lamp of my life has been burned out for Thee

One day, *Dear Daughters*, just like everyone else, your hours will be up; the span of your life on earth will end. Then you will stand before the righteous Judge, and only what matters, only the eternal, only what is done with your heart in the right place will stand at the end. Until then, may our prayer be:

> So teach us to number our days,
> That we may present to You a heart of wisdom.
> (Psalm 90:12)

On that day, nothing else will have mattered. So, what else would we do? Success doesn't look like what you think. Only chase what matters.

> You shall love the LORD your God with all your heart and with all your soul and with all your might. (Deuteronomy 6:5)

CHAPTER FIVE

Dear Daughters,

Being a woman doesn't mean your emotions overrun your intelligence. You can and should think deeply.

I once heard someone say you can miss heaven by eighteen inches. What was meant was you can have head knowledge about Jesus, but never know Him in your heart. While that might be true, it wasn't made as a kind statement of warning. In fact, it wasn't nice at all. Rather, it was meant to slight someone who desired to seriously, deeply know the Truth of Christ. It was meant to relay the false message that following Christ is strictly an emotional endeavor and that any desire to intellectually consider Him would lead to pride, legalism, or a false faith that equaled that of a Pharisee.

In our modern culture, and I'm afraid, in the Church today, there is a growing battle for the mind. Faith is often portrayed as mindless or something to be felt, and not something that can be contemplated, studied, or understood with our intellect. Matters of faith are being devalued to matters of emotion or experience and are considered relative, superstitious, abstract, and even ignorant. Meanwhile, matters of science or "reality" are considered measurable, verifiable, and concrete.

Regrettably, Christians are fueling this perception, both in what we say and in what we don't. Popular songs comparing our faith to falling in love or to a romantic kiss display the growing movement across today's Christianity implying our feelings should lead our faith. You hear Christians claiming to be "on fire for God," and others dismissing previously held beliefs because something didn't "feel right" to them, and still others pushing for people to stop worrying about church doctrine and "just love Jesus."

We will fiercely defend our belief in a miraculously born Savior, who is resurrected from the dead (which are radically absurd assertions), yet at the same time, we're largely silent on issues of creation, the reliability of the Bible, and the exclusivity of the Gospel.

Our churches are filled with songs about the goodness of our God, as well they should be, but shy away from discussions about why a "good" God would allow such evil in our world. The world regards our silence as weakness and our faith as an emotional crutch for the simple-minded. Meanwhile, our fallback answer has become a shrug while saying, "I just take it on faith," or "You just have to have faith." Maybe the most discouraging thing happening in the Church is that those who *are* looking for the truth are often labeled judgmental, unloving, and self-righteous.

The idea that the Christian faith is more about feeling than believing is widespread. It's affirmed by men and women in churches across the world, but it might be most prevalent among women. If we're not careful, our modern Christian expression will be driven by emotional responses and experiential events, instead of true Bible study and exposition. It seems we want a faith that can stir us, encourage us, motivate us, confirm and validate us, but we want our faith to be in something we can *feel* and *experience*, instead of a truth to know and respond to.

Dear Daughters, being a woman doesn't mean emotions overrun your intelligence. You can and should think deeply. While we do operate in faith, it's *not* a blind faith. It's *not* an uninformed faith. Our faith is based on the Truth, and the Truth will always stand. As believers, we should engage our minds to thoughtfully and truthfully consider, evaluate, and deeply study God's Truth.

Not a New Notion

Throughout history, women have been singled out as the emotional gender. The word "hysteria," which is widely defined as unmanageable excessive emotion, originates from the Greek word for "uterus," as it was thought to appear only in women.[22] This common diagnosis was used as a defense for keeping women out of politics and certain professions because we were thought to be unable to control our character, too easily swayed by our emotions.

Sadly, though the medical diagnosis of hysteria has vanished, the thought that women are ruled by our feelings has not. In a Gallup poll[23] of over 1,000 adults, 90 percent of participants said they believed the characteristic "emotional" applied more to women than to men. Mark Driscoll, in his book on church leadership, said, "Before you get all emotional like a woman in hearing this . . ."[24] implying that women are slower to or hindered from coming to biblical conclusions because of our emotional responses.

Worse yet, it has long been thought that women are the weaker sex in regard to intellect. Charles Darwin wrote that men can attain "a higher eminence, in whatever he takes up, than can women—whether requiring deep thought, reason, or imagination, or merely the use of the senses and hands."[25] A devout follower of Darwin's, George Romanes, said evolution is continuing to cause females to become "increasingly less cerebral and more emotional."[26] Gustave Le Bon said of women, "They excel in fickleness, inconsistency, absence of thought and logic, and incapacity to reason. Without a doubt there exist some distinguished women, very superior to the average man but they are as exceptional as the birth of any monstrosity, as, for example, of a gorilla with two heads; consequently, we may neglect them entirely."[27]

This misperception hasn't gone anywhere. In Saudi Arabia, where women are banned from driving, a cleric recently claimed that the ban should continue because women only have half the intellect of men.[28] A recent study by a psychologist at the University of Illinois revealed that children as young as six are already shaped by the stereotype that men are smarter than women.[29] In 1992, the resentment rose swiftly when Mattel released Teen Talk Barbie, who spoke phrases such as, "Will we ever have enough clothes?" "Wouldn't you love to be a lifeguard?" "Wanna go shopping?" and "Math class is tough."[30] A national women's group accused Mattel of bolstering the stereotype that girls aren't as capable as boys in math and science.[31]

Have We Sold Ourselves Short?

The question is, have we, as women, bought into these stereotypes? Are we embracing an uninformed, emotional faith? Have we been stifled into a faith that is shallow?

Women might allow our emotions to overrun our intelligence for several reasons:

♥ ♥ ♥♥

♥ The culture has led us to believe that we're primarily emotional and thus somehow less capable of serious thinking.

♥ Cultural prejudices have not afforded us the same opportunities for study and theological education.

♥ We have been content to be satisfied with sporadic emotional and experiential highs due to our desire for instant gratification.

Growing up, I heard this referred to as the "camp high," not realizing I was not being prepared for the effort and consistency necessary for a deep, considerate knowledge of God.

♥ False teachings and false teachers have led us to this shallow view of our Christian faith.

♥ Any attempt to think deeply and study diligently has been met with opposition, or we have had difficulty finding solid biblical teaching, so we give up.

♥ We have committed so much of our time and efforts to so many other things—even good things—that we believe we cannot commit to the diligent study of His Word.

Whatever our reasons, the results remain. Women in the church are struggling with shallow faiths and shipwrecked walks. We have become prone to false teachings and are being led astray. Discernment only comes when we study the truth enough to recognize the false. And worst of all, when we allow our emotions to distract us from seriously and consistently contemplating God according to His Word, we're missing the marvelous, majestic glory of who He truly is.

Emotions Are Real

Don't misunderstand—emotions are very real. We feel. We cry. We laugh. We fear. We love. We are emotional beings, and that is by God's design. As people, we respond to our experiences and our circumstances. What we have to be on guard against is letting those emotions, those responses overrun our minds or determine our behaviors.

> When we allow our emotions to distract us from seriously and consistently contemplating God according to His Word, we're missing the marvelous, majestic glory of who He truly is.

As missionary Elisabeth Elliot so eloquently put it: "The difficulty is to keep a tight reign on our emotions. They may remain, but it is not they who are to rule the action. They have no authority. A life lived in God is not lived on the plane of the feelings, but of the will. In Scripture the heart is the will—the man himself, the spring of all action, the ruling power bestowed on him by his Creator, capable of choosing and acting."[32] Elliot also warned against allowing our emotions to rob us of authentic worship. "Worship is not an experience. Worship is an act, and this takes discipline. We are to worship 'in spirit and in truth.' Never mind about the feelings. We are to worship in spite of them."[33]

Authentic worship is founded in reality, and it cannot be dependent on emotions or feelings. No circumstances can strip away true faith or hinder true worship.

True Knowledge Leads to True Faith

So, what is the remedy? Go to God's Word. In the Bible, we find this account:

Jesus answered, "The foremost is, 'HEAR, O ISRAEL! THE LORD OUR GOD IS ONE LORD; AND YOU SHALL LOVE THE LORD YOUR GOD WITH ALL YOUR HEART, AND WITH ALL YOUR SOUL, AND WITH ALL YOUR MIND, AND WITH ALL YOUR STRENGTH." (Mark 12:29–30)

Here, a man who was trying to trap Jesus asked Him what commandment was foremost. Jesus restated this command from the Old Testament Law, except "mind" was not in the original commandment. Jesus included "mind," and this version is found in Matthew, Mark, and Luke. The word translated "mind" is the Greek word *dianoia,* which translates thought, understanding, intellect. It carries the meaning of critical thinking or thorough reasoning. "Love" is the Greek word *agapao,* and it means to love *dearly* or to prefer. When used with God or Christ, it involves the thought of affectionate reverence and obedience.

Jesus, Himself, says we are to love Him by using all our intellect. He directs us to approach Him with critical thinking. Our worship—our affectionate reverence and obedience—is to be done with thorough reasoning. In fact, our worship becomes deeper as we worship God with the fullness of our minds. The more profoundly we consider His character, His deeds, and His worthiness, the more heartfelt our belief in Him will become. Our praise will follow.

We find a similar truth taught in Paul's letter to the Roman believers. Speaking to Christians, he says it's when we become "obedient from the heart to that form of teaching to which [we] were committed" (Romans 6:17) that we're freed from slavery to sin and become slaves of righteousness. When our hearts embrace God's truth, we are freed.

Later, when he is expressing his deep desire for all of Israel to be saved, Paul says he can testify to their zeal—their passion, ardor, and fervent spirit—but that it's "not in accordance with knowledge" (Romans 10:2). Paul regrets they had a passion but were missing knowledge.

The Gospel of John tells us about another group of people, the Samaritans, who worshiped without correct and full knowledge of the object of their worship. Jesus said, "true worshipers will worship the Father in spirit and truth" (John 4:23). Problems start and a false faith exists when we try to worship apart from knowledge or with disengaged minds.

God's Word is clear. Worship begins with what we know about Christ from the truth of His Word and springs up from there. Colossians 3:16 says it this way: "Let the word of Christ richly dwell within you, with all wisdom teaching and admonishing one another with psalms *and* hymns *and* spiritual songs, singing with thankfulness in your hearts to God." When we're filled with the knowledge of who God is, and His Word richly dwells in us, our love for Him and our worship of Him will grow. True knowledge leads to true faith. Greater knowledge leads to greater faith.

Think Deeply

God's Word urges believers—all believers—to "be transformed by the renewing of your mind, so that you may prove what the will of God is, that which is good and acceptable and perfect" (Romans 12:2). The Greek word translated "mind" in this verse is *noos,* and it means the faculty of perceiving and understanding. This is the part of us that has the capacity to think and reason and to execute reflective thinking. We can think about what we're thinking and what

> *True knowledge leads to true faith. Greater knowledge leads to greater faith.*

has happened to make us think that way. The word "renewing" is from the Greek *nakainosei*, which means completing, making fresh or new, or renovating. Our Christian walks are to be directed by minds that perceive properly. Our minds then direct our service and worship of God, according to His will. Our faith in the one true God is not an empty, mindless endeavor, but rather a thoughtful, mindful pursuit. The Lord doesn't command something from us that we're not capable of doing. He makes it clear. He wants our minds and our hearts.

God has blessed humans with both emotions and intelligence. We can think *and* feel. True worship, real faith according to the Bible, is known when we fully engage *both* our minds and our hearts. Just look at the woman in the seventh chapter of Luke. Jesus had been invited to dine with a Pharisee. The Bible says a woman, a sinner, who had heard Jesus was to dine at the Pharisee's table came with a precious alabaster vial of perfume. She stood at Jesus' feet, weeping—so much so that her tears fell from her face and wet His feet.

As she wiped His feet with her own hair, kissing them and anointing them with her perfume, the Pharisee only saw an emotional mess from a sinful woman. But Jesus saw through to her heart. He saw a woman who knew her sin, who knew who He was, and knowing both, extravagantly worshiped her Savior. She worshiped Him because she knew. And what was the Messiah's response to her? "Your faith has saved you; go in peace" (Luke 7:50).

Just like this woman, when we contemplate His forgiveness of our many sins, we will love Him with all our heart, soul, strength, and mind, and that faith will save us. We will worship because we know.

Closing the Gap

Emotions are important; they are given to us by God. But they must not rule our intellect. Our emotions must be based on the truth of God's Word. We must not place our faith or trust in our emotions or our feelings. Our faith must be in the Lord. *Dear Daughters*, being a woman doesn't mean emotions overrun your intelligence. You can and should think deeply. The truth is, when we seek to know God as He has revealed Himself in His Word, and when we choose to contemplate His character and His deeds, we end up with a wonderfully rich balance of the intellectual and the emotional. The more we get to know God, the more we will love Him. Our head and our heart will align.

CHAPTER SIX

Dear Daughters,

Sex is Awesome—When You Follow God's Design

Full confession; I did not want to write this letter. I would rather accidentally stick my forehead into the meringue of a pie and have my picture taken again, or be called on to locate Spain on a map in front of my whole sixth grade social studies class again, or sing and dance on stage while dressed like a turkey being chased by a cook with an axe (some embarrassments just stick with you), than to willingly bring up this topic with my daughters. And yet, here we are.

You may be asking yourself, as I am, "Well, then *why* are you bringing it up?" Here's the truth—I am bringing it up because I refuse to remain silent and relinquish my responsibility to a world that continues to twist the standards. I am bringing it up because I honestly believe that nothing has as much stigma, as much false information, and as much false expectation attached to it as does sex, and some of that is the fault of the Church. The subject is misused, mishandled, and misunderstood. It's exploited, distorted, and devalued.

Looking around at our world today, I believe nothing has as much potential for harm and hurt. And yet, looking at God's Word, I believe nothing has as much possibility for blessings and beauty. So, let's talk about it. Because, *Dear Daughters,* sex is awesome when you follow God's design.

Sex Was God's Idea

If you want to truly understand God's design for sex, you need to go back to where it all began. When God created Eve, He brought her to Adam as his counterpart, his equal opposite, flesh of his flesh. He created them as male and female, and He blessed them and told them to "be fruitful and multiply" (Genesis 1:28). God sets the standard from the very beginning: "For this reason a man shall leave his father and his mother, and be joined to his wife; and they shall become one flesh" (Genesis 2:24).

Man was to be joined, to become one flesh with his wife, his counterpart, and together, they would be fruitful. The Bible says that God *blessed* them in this. God's design for the physical act of sex and the family unit that it produces is a blessing given to us by our Creator God.

The Bible also says, "the man and his wife were both naked and were not ashamed" (Genesis 2:25). Before sin, Adam and his wife, Eve, were free to enjoy the blessing of sex without any shame. Remember that when God had completed His creation, which included sex, He pronounced it all "very good." It's obvious that from the beginning, God created sex to be a beautiful kindness for His greatest and treasured creation.

God's Design for Sex

Sex was created by God, and, therefore, in His design, it's not wrong, shameful, demeaning, dirty, or detrimental. In fact, the opposite is true. While those who hold to the biblical standards for sex are often labeled prudish or stifled, the truth is that understanding and embracing God's design for sex will lead to a vibrant and enjoyable view of sexuality and its awesomeness.

Fruit of the Womb

Sex is awesome because God designed it for pro-creation in marriage. While this is, by no means, the only purpose for it, it's likely the most obvious. It cannot be denied that God fashioned humans to reproduce sexually. The Bible is clear, and any parent can declare that one of the biggest blessings of sex is the children who are born.

Behold, children are a gift of the LORD,
The fruit of the womb is a reward.
Like arrows in the hand of a warrior,
So are the children of one's youth.
How blessed is the man whose quiver is full of them.
(Psalm 127:3-5a)

How astounding that this extraordinary act of intimacy brings forth the blessing of a new life—a being who bears the image of God who will live on forever. Two things do need to be clarified here. The first is that God does not command all fertile, married couples to have as many children as physically possible. The number and spacing of children should be agreed upon by both parents, only after seeking God's wisdom. The second is that God has a plan for sex for infertile couples as well, though it might not include procreation. And should you ever find yourself struggling with the pain of infertility, know this: the Lord loves you, He holds you *dear*, and He is your strength and your trust.

Stick Like Glue

Sex is awesome because God designed it to create a powerful, unifying bond in the marriage. In Matthew 19:4-6, Jesus spoke about marriage, and He restated and applied Genesis 2:24-25:

Have you not read that He who created *them* from the beginning MADE THEM MALE AND FEMALE, and said 'FOR THIS REASON A MAN SHALL LEAVE HIS FATHER AND MOTHER AND BE JOINED TO HIS WIFE, AND THE TWO SHALL BECOME ONE FLESH'? So they are no longer two, but one flesh. What therefore God has joined together, let no man separate.

Jesus confirms that God's design for marriage is for one man and one woman to be joined together. The word "joined" means to cleave, glue together, cement, fasten, and hold fast. The same meaning is used when we're told to cling to or hold on to God. The Hebrew word translated "flesh" is *basar,* and means body or person. What the Father has said, and what Jesus confirmed, is that the call and design for marriage is for a man and a woman to cleave together as one organism or one unit, now indivisible.

This joining process includes sex, but it's not limited to sex. Sex by itself does not make or break a marriage, but it's designed to help bond a man and woman. When a husband and wife come together physically, this bond, this joining is strengthened in the most intimate way. The act of sex not only bonds us physically, but also chemically, mentally, and emotionally. God actually created sex to be a powerful "super glue" to increase the stability of marriage over time.

We can clearly see this when such bonds are made in sexual relationships and then broken. Following the breakup of an intimate relationship, people often encounter a wide range of severe emotions and experience emotional damage. There are physical, emotional, and spiritual ramifications, and those consequences are far-reaching. In His infinite knowledge, God knew marriages would be difficult from time to time. He established sex to be an act that would bolster our covenants and draw us into a deeper, richer, closer, more affectionate relationship with each other.

Wedded Bliss

Sex is awesome because God designed it for our pleasure. When God said everything He had created was "very good," that included sex and the pleasure that comes from it. It's a gift from Him. Sex is designed to be thrilling, fun, enjoyable. The idea that God is some uptight party-pooper who's out to ruin all our fun doesn't sync with the God who intentionally created erogenous zones and the orgasm. He wanted us to enjoy sex, and so He made it incredibly satisfying.

Our good God intended sex to be experienced within the safe boundaries of marriage. It's in this committed, secure relationship that He gave us the freedom to revel in the pleasure of sex. In Proverbs 5:18–19, God wisely counsels men to:

Rejoice in the wife of your youth.
As a loving hind and a graceful doe,
Let her breasts satisfy you at all times;
Be exhilarated always with her love.

Song of Solomon is a love poem between King Solomon and his bride, and there is no doubt that they both delighted in the God-given, God-honoring desire they had for one another.

Here's an important question: What if sex isn't enjoyable for you? This is where the beauty of being in a committed covenant relationship shines. You get to be vulnerable here. You get to communicate your deepest desires and your needs here. But you're going to have to commit to taking charge of your own sexuality and being open with the man you married, trusting that it's God's desire for you to find pleasure together. I believe this is where part of the false expectations and misunderstandings about sex wreak havoc on our marriages. Women seem to be under the impression, and I'm sure some have promoted the idea, that sex is for men. But studies show that husbands are more satisfied when they have a satisfied wife. If you feel like you're just there to service your husband or check something off a list, think again. Statistics show that he wants to please you, too.

Other serious issues can hinder pleasure during sex, such as marital conflicts, body image issues, broken trusts, past sexual abuse, and issues with pain. If you find yourself struggling in any of these areas, prayer, seeking godly wisdom, and communicating honestly with each other is paramount. As a couple, you may need to speak with a trusted pastor or friend who will give you biblical advice, or you might need to see a doctor. Whatever you do, know that it's not scriptural to just let it slide. There will be times when it's not physically possible to enjoy sexual pleasure together, but if it is possible and you're still not enjoying it, then you need to address it.

Take hope, your Creator God wants your marriage to be blissful. He is glorified when a married couple desire to please one another and rejoice in their sensuality. Our good God created sex to be a pleasure to His creation.

". . . As I have loved you" (John 13:34)

Sex is awesome because God designed it to shape us to be more like Him. More than procreation, more than a bond, and more than pleasure, God created sex to be a God-honoring expression of self-sacrificial love in the marriage relationship and a reflection of His character.

> But because of immoralities, each man is to have his own wife, and each woman is to have her own husband. The husband must fulfill his duty to his wife, and likewise also the wife to her husband. The wife does not have authority over her own body, but the husband *does*; and likewise also the husband does not have authority over his own body, but the wife *does*. Stop depriving one another, except by agreement for a time, so that you may devote yourselves to prayer, and come together again so that Satan will not tempt you because of your lack of self-control. (1 Corinthians 7:2–5)

Here is part of Paul's letter to the church in Corinth. It's in response to questions previously sent to him regarding sexual immoralities the Corinthian church was participating in. The word "immoralities" comes from the Greek word *porneia*, and it literally translates "surrendering of sexual purity." This is the same root word for the English word "pornography," and it can include anything: illicit sex, fornication, homosexuality, adultery, incest, harlotry, bestiality, etc. God's Word says that because these temptations exist, the husband and wife are to have each other. It's clear that both the husband and the wife have a duty—a debt—to the other that they are to fulfill.

God says that in marriage, you give over the authority of your own body to your spouse for the sexual satisfaction of the other and to help that person resist temptation into sexual sin. The Bible gives direction for the frequency of sex within a marriage, too. It wisely counsels spouses to stop depriving each other—literally keeping sex away from, cheating, or robbing of sex—and to only refrain for an agreed upon time. The Lord, in His wisdom and care for us, gives us parameters for sex within marriage, remembering "our frame . . . that we are *but* dust" (Psalm 103:14).

Our sex lives are to be given and lived out in love. Not just any love, but agape love. Agape love is the same love with which we're to love God. It's a love that prefers one over everyone else, that puts another before anyone else—even yourself. It's a love of service and adoration. In other words, it should be our ambition and our joy to sacrificially out-serve, out-give, and out-do our spouse in every area of our marriage, including our sex life. In fact, God *calls* both husbands and wives to love like this in marriage. And, here's the thing—it's not dependent on the other person. It's a matter of faithful submission to our Lord.

These are Biblical directions for marriage, from God, the Creator of marriage. They apply to both genders. Either spouse disregarding these directions is committing a sin. Selfishness has no place in your sex life. Sex is not simply a physical release. It cannot be an afterthought. Sex is an opportunity to serve, give, and love our spouse to the honor and glory of our Lord.

Agape love is the love Jesus has for us. He put us before Himself, served us, gave everything for us, and loves us self-sacrificially. His actions toward us were not dependent on us but instead were done in His faithful submission to the Father. Jesus tells us to love one another, just as He has loved us. Agape love is the highest expression of love. When we love like that, we look more like Jesus.

Keeping It Holy

Did you ever think you would see sex described as holy? If not, then I ask you to stick with me for a minute. The word "holy" means set apart, sacred, separate, distinct, not to be profaned, pure, undefiled, intended for God's special purpose. God desires for our sex life to be just that—pure, set apart for His purpose, holy.

How can we keep sex holy? This, like every other area of our life, really comes down to a matter of trust. It's a matter of having faith in God's character, understanding that His standards are to secure the very best for us. It's a matter of truly believing that what God has for us is better than what the world can offer, better than what we could ever come up with. If we're actually convinced of that, then we will see His direction and His design as the better plan. Embracing that truth, we will choose to obey Him with a willing, trusting heart.

If you decide to commit yourself to keep sex holy, the blueprint is the same. Whether single, dating, or married, you're going to need to be resolved, fixing your mind ahead of time. You must be decided on the boundaries for sexual purity long before you get anywhere near them. You must keep yourself out of situations that would threaten your self-control. If you push the line, you will fail. God warns against being morally reckless. In 1 Corinthians, the apostle Paul tells believers to "flee" immorality. The Greek word is in the tense that makes it mean to flee and keep on fleeing. It literally means to escape from, as in escaping danger, to take flight, or to run away from. Remember that immorality is anything that you participate in that surrenders your sexual purity. The Lord tells us to escape and keep on escaping the danger of any situation that would tempt us to give over our sexual purity.

Another aspect of keeping sex holy is to have a biblical understanding of that which God has made you a steward. God gave *you* the gift of having sex with your husband. No other person on the planet has been given that same privilege. It is distinctly your gift. The flip side of that is that the *only* sex life he can enjoy, biblically, is the one that you, as his wife, *choose* to give to him. He cannot be naked in front of anyone else and not be ashamed. He cannot be sexually intimate with anyone else and not be regretful. He cannot even look upon or fantasize about anyone but you without it being immoral. *Only you*.

If you ever tire of your husband's sex drive, you need to look at his sexual advances for what they really are. The intimacy and connection of sex—he *wants* those with *you*. Consider his desire for you a wonderful compliment instead of an obligation or something to dread. Recognize that your husband wants to satisfy you and build and foster a great sex life with *you*. What a gift to embrace, and what a blessing to be to your husband! And, you get to take pleasure in the truth that he, by God's design, gets to be the same for you. *That's* something worth waiting for. *That's* something to embrace. *That's* something to hold *dear*. *That's* something to keep holy.

God meant sex to be beautiful. The thing about the beautiful, the good, and the holy is that Satan always attacks it, seeking to deface it, to leave it in ruins. It has been happening since the Garden. He tries to take all things and make them ugly, cheap, and vile. Satan is the destroyer, the liar, the thief.

At his leading, the world is trying to pull all this apart. It will try to say that what we see, hear, and do is no big deal and no one's business. Satan slanders God's character by trying to make His boundaries seem stifling, rather than freeing. He tries to create doubt in our minds about God's good and perfect plan, and he tries to tempt us to follow our own desires instead. Do not be fooled. Know God. Remember His character. Trust in Him and walk out your faith in Him in obedience. Then you can exult in the sensational sex life He wants for you, and know it is holy.

What If I've Already Messed Up?

The truth is, we *all* have some sexual sin. Whether it's lust, deliberately causing another to sin, sex outside of marriage, adultery, homosexuality, or any other immorality, we're all guilty, all broken. Just like all sin, sexual immorality is really another sign of a lack of trust and faith in God. We're effectively saying that He hasn't given us enough in His design, and so we take matters into our own hands. The sad truth is, we do this at our own peril and our own pain. Consequences of disobedience are real. We all know it to be true.

When we surrender our sexual purity, we can suffer physically, mentally, and emotionally. Still, the most agonizing consequences of sexual immorality are the spiritual repercussions. We cause spiritual damage as we carry the name of Christ into sexually immoral situations, hindering our own witness and slandering His character. Our sin also grieves our holy God, causing Him to be righteously angry and sad about our lack of faith in Him. Without repentance that is swift and sincere, our walks with Christ are derailed, and we suffer from the guilt, shame and regret, and on and on it goes.

> *The best part of all of this is that when we have messed it all up, there is a Savior who has paid the price for our sin.*

This is what Satan wants. It's why he twists and deceives. Satan wants us to sink deeper and deeper into the mire and the muck of sin. He wants us to wallow in our rebellion and in the embarrassment and chaos that it brings. He wants to destroy us.

But—rather, instead—God's mercy is more. You see, the best part of all of this is that when we have messed it all up, there is a Savior who has paid the price for our sin. His mercy is more. When we speak of mercy—not receiving the punishment that is due—we also have to speak of God's justice.

It's not that He just erases our sin as if it never happened; that wouldn't be just. Sin has to be punished, and the punishment for sin is death. No, God doesn't ignore our sin and the punishment it earns; He poured it out—on Jesus Christ. Because Jesus took the full wrath of God that we deserved for our sin, God can extend His great mercy to us. All that is required of us is faith—not in ourselves or our ability to earn or somehow deserve salvation, but in Jesus alone. We have faith in the finished work of Christ on Calvary, where His blood was shed for the forgiveness of our sin. When we trust in Him, He pulls us out of the mire and sets our feet on the Rock.

Church, we need to get loud about the truth of God's design for sex!

The key to mercy is to recognize and admit our sin—our deliberate disobedience to the Lord. Godly sorrow over our sin leads us to repent, to change our mind about it, and turn away. God promises us that, "If we confess our sins, He is faithful and righteous to forgive us our sins and to cleanse us from all unrighteousness" (1 John 1:9). *All* unrighteousness.

Having done that and standing in forgiveness, now set your eyes back on Christ. Seek to honor His name and to trust Him enough to obey Him. His plan and His purpose for everything is perfect, and it's for your good.

Time to Speak Out

God's purpose for sex is nothing less than radical. It's radically opposed to the world's views and it goes against our own wants. What if we committed to being women who held the same radical view of sex that God has? What would the impact be on ourselves? On our husbands? On our children? On the lost? What if people could tell that we were followers of Christ by our holy sex lives? Church, we need to get loud about the truth of God's design for sex! This world sure is loud in their lies, and when we let them drown us out and deceive us, we're robbing ourselves of His good and perfect gift.

Be certain that God's desire is for sex to be a blessing to our marriages, not a burden. It's to help strengthen our covenant, not stress it. It's to be our delight, not our dismay. If you find yourself struggling with viewing sex as a burden, a strain, or a disappointment, turn your eyes to the character of the One who created it. His desire is for you and your husband to have an exhilarating, beautiful, holy sex life. Will you trust Him with it? *Dear Daughters*, sex is awesome when you follow God's design.

CHAPTER SEVEN

Dear Daughters,

*Jesus is
everything!*

This could have been the first letter I wrote. In fact, *every* letter could have been titled, "Jesus is Everything!" Because all this—seeking to *know* God, desiring to obey and honor God by following His direction in *all* areas, wanting to live with purpose, chasing only what truly matters, seeking to think deeply about Him and His truths, loving and worshiping Him with all our heart, soul, strength, and mind—is rooted in this one truth. Jesus is everything!

If you put this letter down, and you remember nothing else, remember this: Jesus truly is everything! He's it.

Be sure . . .
- ♥ He is the Creator of all things. Colossians 1:16 says, "for by Him all things were created."
- ♥ He is the Sustainer of all things. Colossians 1:17 says, "in Him all things hold together."
- ♥ He is the Savior who redeems all things. Colossians 1:20 says, "and through Him to reconcile all things to Himself, having made peace through the blood of His cross."
- ♥ If you're wondering, He is the Truth—the only truth—absolute and sure.
- ♥ If you're lost, He is the Way—the only way to be right with our holy God.

- ❥ If you're dead in your sins, He is the Life—life that is abundant now and eternal: everlasting (John 14:6).
- ❥ He is the Promise of God, Himself—the Christ, the Messiah. Matthew 16:16 says, "You are the Christ, the Son of the living God."
- ❥ He is our Hope—our only Hope. 1 Timothy 1:1 says, ". . . Christ Jesus, *who is* our hope."
- ❥ He is the Righteous Judge, judging with impartiality and without bias, the only one whose opinion will matter in the end. John 5:22 says, ". . . but He has given all judgment to the Son."
- ❥ He is our Mediator, our true Advocate. Do you need a women's advocate? You have the true Advocate in Jesus. 1 Timothy 2:5 says, "For there is one God, *and* one mediator also between God and men, *the* man Christ Jesus."
- ❥ He is our Lord, the greatest King, the Ruler of all things. Revelation 19:16 says, "And on His robe and on His thigh He has a name written, 'KING OF KINGS, AND LORD OF LORDS.'"
- ❥ He is our Reward. Revelation 2:28 says, "and I will give him the morning star."
- ❥ He is the Author and Finisher of our faith, truly everything that we believe in. Hebrews 12:2 says, "fixing our eyes on Jesus, the author and perfecter of faith."

Jesus is truly everything!

Be sure . . .

Jesus is all-knowing and all-powerful, self-sacrificial, and merciful. He is the Great Shepherd. He's forgiving and full of grace. He loves without provocation and without end. He is our Comforter, our Friend, our Rock, and our Refuge.

Jesus is everything!

Be sure . . .

Jesus is our Kinsman Redeemer, the One—the only One—who paid our debt in full. He's the Name above all names. He is our trust and our Salvation. He is our Soon-Coming King, and He's worthy of all praise and all honor and all glory.

Jesus is everything!

And *Dear Daughters*, it is my prayer that you would *receive* Him. John 1:12 says, "But as many as received Him, to them He gave the right to become children of God." The greatest thing that you could ever do, the greatest thing anyone could ever do is to receive Jesus Christ as your Lord and Savior.

But my prayer is that you would not just receive Him, but that you would *know* Him. According to Jesus' own words in John 17:3, we can know

Him. We can know His nature. We can know His character. We can know *Him*. He wants us to know Him, so He has revealed the truth of who He is in His Word.

But more than that, we cannot only know Him, but we can *walk with* Him. John 15 tells us to abide with Him—to walk with Him, which means we would consider Him in our day-to-day lives at every turn. Galatians 2:20 says that when we receive Christ, it's no longer we who live, but Christ who lives in us.

But even greater than walking with Him, my prayer for each one of you is that you would bring Him all the glory He is due. I have no greater joy than to hear that my children—my daughters—are walking in the truth, that their lives, the span of their hours, are bringing glory to our Savior. Because, *dear, dear Daughters*, Jesus is truly everything!

For from Him and through Him and to Him are all things. To Him be the glory forever. Amen.
–Romans 11:36

Notes

Chapter One

♥ *Dear Daughters*, You are oh so special, but you are not enough.

1. Phil Vischer and Mike Nawrocki, *Closing to the Veggie Tales*, Veggie Tales, Big Idea Entertainment (1993–2015).

Chapter Two

♥ *Dear Daughters*, Biblical Christianity doesn't mean you're less than a man in God's plan.

2. John Chrysostum, *The Kind of Women Who Ought to Be Taken as Wives*. Translated by Elizabeth A. Clark. Women in the Early Church, Michael Glazier, Inc. 1983. https://christianhistoryinstitute.org/magazine/article/women-archives-wifes-domain/

3. Saint Augustine, Bishop of Hippo Regius (354–430), quote taken from https://alternet.org/2-13/20-vile-quotes-against-women-religious-leaders-st-augustine-pat-robertson.

4. Ibid.

5. John Calvin, *Commentary on Corinthians, Volume I*, translated by Rev. John Prizile, (Grand Rapids, Michigan: Christian Classics Ethereal Library).

6. John Shelby Spong, *The Sins of Scripture: Exposing the Bible's Texts of Hate to Reveal the God of Love*, (New York, New York: Harper Collins, 2005).

7. Complete Word of Josephus: Antiquities of the Jews, New York: Bigelow, Brown, 1800, Chapter 8.

8. Rabbi Eliezer ben Hyrcanus, in the Mishnah 200 AD and Jerusalem Talmud 500 AD, JT Sotah 3:4, 19a.

9. Glaser, Zhava. "Jesus and the Role of Women." Jews for Jesus (website). June 1, 1988. https://jewsforjesus. org/publications/newsletter/newsletter-jun-1988/jesus-and-the-role-of-women/

Chapter Three

♥ *Dear Daughters,* You will need direction. God's Word is His biggest blessing to you.

10. Gerry Greenstone, MD, "The History of Bloodletting," (*British Columbia Medical Journal*, vol. 52, no.1, Jan/Feb 2010), 12–14.

11. R.J. Reynolds ad. "REWIND: 1949 CIGARETTE SPOT DECLARES 'DOCTORS SMOKE CAMELS,'" https://adage. com/article/news/rewind-1949-cigarette-spot-declares-doctors-smoke-camels/236635. See also "The Doctors' Choice Is America's Choice," https://www.ncbi.nlm.nih. gov/pmc/articles/PMC1470496/.

12. According to the following "Truth Initiative" article, this is a quote from the president of Philip Morris in a 1971 TV interview "The 5 ways tobacco companies lied about the dangers of cigarette smoking," https://truthinitiative. org/research-resources/tobacco-prevention-efforts/5-ways-tobacco-companies-lied-about-dangers-smoking.

13. Taken from a lecture by Cédric Villani, recorded in the article "Cédric Villani delivers public lecture on the 'age of the earth,'" www.icm2018.org/wp/2018/08/06/cedric-villani-delivers-public-lecture-on-the-age-of-the-earth/.

14. Lyrics from hymn are in public domain, hymnary.org/ text/how_firm_a_foundation_ye_saints_of.

Chapter Four

♥ *Dear Daughters,* Success doesn't look like what you think. Only chase what matters.

15. https://www.cia.gov/library/publications/the-world-factbook/geos/xx.html#field-anchor-people-and-society-birth-rate.

16. "Life expectancy at birth, female (years)," https://data.worldbank.org/indicator/SP.DYN.LE00.FE.IN.

17. "Americans hate their jobs and even perks don't help," https://www.today.com/money/americans-hate-their-jobs-even-perks-dont-help-6C10423977.

18. "Antidepressant Use Up 400 Percent in US," https://psychcentral.com/news/2011/10/25/antidepressant-use-up-400-percent-in-us/30677.html.

19. http://www.nimh.nih.gov/health/statistics/suicide.shtml

20. https://www.cdc.gov/nchs/products/databriefs/db76.htm

21. C.T. Studd, "Only One Life," public domain.

Chapter Five

♥ *Dear Daughters*, Being a woman doesn't mean your emotions overrun your intelligence. You can and should think deeply.

22. "Women and Hysteria in the History of Mental Health," https://www.ncbi.nlm.nih.gov/pmc/articles/PMC3480686/. See also https://en.wikipedia.org/wiki/Hysteria.

23. "Americans See Women as Emotional and Affectionate, Men as More Aggressive," https://news.gallup.com/poll/1978/americans-see-women-emotional-affectionate-men-more-aggressive.aspx.

24. Mark Driscoll, *Mark Driscoll, Church Leadership: Explaining the Roles of Jesus, Elders, Deacons, and Members at Mars Hill, Mars Hill Theology Series* (Seattle, Washington: Mars Hill Church, 2004), 43. http://www.dennyburk.com/mark-driscoll-on-women-in-ministry-2/

25. Charles Darwin, *The Descent of Man and Selection in Relation to Sex,* (New York: D. Appleton and Company, 1896), 564.

26. Jerry Bergman Ph.D., "Darwin's Teaching of Women's Inferiority," (Institute for Creation Research, ISR, 1994), www.icr.org/article/darwins-teaching-womens-inferiority/.

27. Stephen Jay Gould, *The Mismeasure of Man*, (New York: W. W. Norton & Company, 1981).

28. "Saudi Arabia's ban on women driving must remain because they 'lack the intellect' of men, says leading cleric," https://www.independent.co.uk/news/world/middle-east/saudi-arabia-woman-driving-ban-remain-lack-intellect-men-sexism-sheikh-saad-al-hajari-islamic-leader-a7960501.html.

29. "Evidence of bias against girls and women in contexts that emphasize intellectual ability," https://psycnet.apa.org/doiLanding?doi=10.1037%2Famp0000427.

30. https://en.wikipedia.org/wiki/Teen_Talk_Barbie.

31. "Mattel Says It Erred; Teen Talk Barbie Turns Silent on Math," https://www.nytimes.com/1992/10/21/business/company-news-mattel-says-it-erred-teen-talk-barbie-turns-silent-on-math.html?scp=1.

32. Elisabeth Elliot (2002), *Quest for Love: True Stories of Passion and Purity*, (Revell, 2002), 35.

33. https://www.goodreads.com/quotes/564689-worship-is-not-an-experience-worship-is-an-act-and.

About the Author

Brenna McLennan has served as a children's minister for more than 10 years, leading a dynamic and fruitful children's ministry. Her passion is to lay an unshakable foundation of Biblical Truth—one that will stand up to the growing avalanche of mistruth and doubt the world heaps on our young people. Brenna is also a gifted ladies' teacher, able to make God's Word accessible and applicable to today's generation of women. She deeply loves her Savior Jesus, and therefore, continually finds herself growing in her love of His Word. Her hope is that many would follow that same pattern. Her heart is that many would be "held back" from the pain and suffering of this world by finding peace in Jesus Christ.

Brenna is married to the love of her life and first grade sweetheart, Tanner, who is a cotton farmer. Brenna and Tanner have four daughters, Maddie, Amy, Maebree, and Adalyn. Their girls are the joy of their crazy days. Brenna's hobbies include reading, tennis, working in her flower bed, and "all good food!"

the Josiah Project
Seeking a Resurgence of Biblical Truth

The Josiah Project is a teaching, preaching, writing
ministry seeking a resurgence of
Biblical Truth in our day. We believe our hope
is a solid turning to the truth of God's Word
and the Savior of that Word—Jesus.

For other resources, to order additional
copies of *Letters to My Daughters*, to book
an event, or to contact us personally, please
look us up at thejosiahproject.net.

"Sanctify them in the truth; Your word is truth."
—John 17:17

Electric Moon Publishing, LLC is a custom, independent publisher who assists indie authors, ministries, businesses, and organizations with their book publishing needs. Services include writing, editing, design, layout, print, e-book, marketing, and distribution. For more information please use the contact form found on www.emoonpublishing.com.